The Sa~~y~~ ~~g~~ ~~~

The Sayings of

MARK
TWAIN

edited by

JAMES MUNSON

DUCKWORTH

First published in 1992 by
Gerald Duckworth & Co. Ltd.
The Old Piano Factory
48 Hoxton Square, London N1 6PB

A catalogue record for this book is available
from the British Library

ISBN 0 7156 2421 0

Photoset in North Wales by
Derek Doyle & Associates, Mold, Clwyd
Printed in Great Britain by
Redwood Press Limited, Melksham

Contents

To
Alex and Patti

Introduction

Samuel Langhorne Clemens, known as Mark Twain, once said that humour was 'mankind's greatest blessing'. If so, those who, like him, see the humour in life and put it into words must be among mankind's greatest benefactors. He was born in 1835 in Missouri, a state then on the western frontier of the American South. Geography is a key to understanding Twain: Missouri was a border state between North and South. It also stood between the settled East and the vacant West. These conflicts and the awesome majesty of the Mississippi River, which formed Missouri's eastern border and on whose banks Twain grew up, sparked his genius as a writer. When he drew on these two sources, his genius flowered and he was regarded, in his time and since, as the quintessentially *American* writer. Of his own writing he said: 'I have never tried ... to help cultivate the cultivated classes. I was not equipped for it ... and I never had any ambition in that direction.' His goal was to write for 'bigger game – the masses'.

The frontier world in which he grew up is the basis for his most famous books, *The Adventures of Tom Sawyer* and *The Adventures of Huckleberry Finn*. He was apprenticed as a printer and then became a steamboat pilot on the Mississippi. When the War Between the States began, Missouri was torn between rival state governments and the division was shown in Twain's own life: after serving briefly, first with the Southern and then with the Northern side, he fled the war and went west to Nevada. Here he turned to journalism and first used the pen-name Mark Twain (the cry which Mississippi boatmen used to indicate the depth of the river, in this case, two fathoms). His time in the West produced his famous story 'The Celebrated Jumping Frog of Calaveras County', and later his book, *Roughing It*, a narrative of his adventures.

Twain made his name as a writer with his 1867 travel book *Innocents Abroad*, describing the often hilarious exploits of the first organised American tour of Europe. In 1870 he married Miss Olivia Langdon, daughter of an established and wealthy New York family, and other travel books, novels and essays followed. In those years of political corruption, unparalleled in American history, he turned his back on the South and identified with the victorious North, for which he wrote. In the 1870s and 1880s he brought out his best known works: *Tom Sawyer, Huckleberry Finn, A Tramp Abroad, The Prince and the Pauper, A Connecticut Yankee in King Arthur's Court* and *Life on the Mississippi*.

Disaster struck, however, in 1894 when an unwise investment plunged Twain into bankruptcy. Despite his cynical or, to some, realistic view of man's nature, he set out to repay his debts. He toured the world and came back to produce essays and books which included *Following the Equator, The Tragedy of Pudd'nhead Wilson, The Personal Recollections of Joan of Arc, The American Claimant, Tom Sawyer Abroad, Tom Sawyer, Detective* and *The Man that Corrupted Hadleyburg*, all published in the 1890s. He worked into the new century and produced several works which drew on his 'dark side'. He had long believed, as he said in *Following the Equator*, that 'Everything human is pathetic. The secret source of Humor itself is not joy but sorrow. There is no humor in heaven.' *The Man that Corrupted Hadleyburg, What Is Man?* and *The Mysterious Stranger* (published after his death) all display a bitterness and determinism present in earlier works but not stated with such force. Twain was also beset by a succession of personal tragedies: in 1896 his daughter Susy died, followed in 1904 by his wife and in 1909 by his daughter Jean.

By the end of his life Twain was a national institution, a prophet whose biting witticisms were eagerly sought – much as George Bernard Shaw's were in the decades that followed. In Britain, he has always been a popular and much quoted writer, and there was no distinction he cherished more than his honorary Oxford doctorate. In 1906 he began dictating to his devoted secretary, Albert Bigelow Paine, material for his posthumously published *Biography* and *Autobiography*, and these remain two of the greatest quarries for his witticisms. In 1909 he told Paine: 'I came in with Halley's comet in 1835. It is coming again next year, and I expect to go out with it. It will be the greatest disappointment of my life if I don't go out with Halley's comet. The Almighty has said, no doubt: "Now, here are these two unaccountable freaks; they came in together,

they must go out together." ' Twain's wish was granted:
the comet appeared on 20 April 1910 and on the following
day he died.

Novelist, travel writer, humorist, essayist, speaker,
raconteur, satirist, wit: all these describe Twain. As a writer
of fiction his fame is securely founded on his novels of life
on the Southern frontier. As a humorist and composer of
maxims and quips, his reputation rests on his anecdotal or
'folksy' manner, a style known in America as 'cracker
barrel'. Its lack of education cannot conceal its inherent
wisdom, a wisdom based on Everyman's own experience
of life. The approach recalls Benjamin Franklin's maxims in
Poor Richard's Almanack. Although they have an 'off-hand'
or casual manner and, indeed, are sometimes best read
with a Southern drawl, they are by no means impromptu.
Twain's manuscripts show that he worked on his witticisms, and frequently rewrote them.

Twain based much of his humour on that essentially
American trait of laughing at those who put on airs. His
maxims can still make us uncomfortable because, hidden
within the humour, there is a clear observation of human
nature. 'Laughter without a tinge of philosophy,' Twain
wrote, 'is but a sneeze of humor. Genuine humor is replete
with wisdom.' It is only laughter that can blow a 'colossal
humbug' to 'rags and atoms at a blast. Against the assault
of laughter nothing can stand.' His humour always had an
underpinning of despair at man's capacity for self-
deception and hypocrisy.

Despite Twain's literary fame and the social acceptance
his wife brought him, he was always to some degree a
naughty but clever schoolboy sneaking a free look at the
human circus that had come to town. He always lacked
that calm acceptance of the status quo which a steady
advance through life gives a man. His dark side is not so
much a product of the despair which beset him in old age
as part of his very nature as a writer. But let Mark Twain
have the final word. 'Ah, well,' he once told Paine, 'I am a
great and sublime fool. But then I am God's fool, and all
His work must be contemplated with respect.'

Sources

The following books were used to compile this selection. The abbreviation is given first, followed by the full details. Where several editions are available, only chapter references are given. Unless noted otherwise, all books were published in New York. An asterisk marks editions in Twain's 1899 collected Author's National Edition:

Works by Mark Twain

American Claimant = *The American Claimant, Etc.**

Bequest = *The $30,000 Bequest, Etc.**

Calaveras County = [J. Paul, ed.], *The Celebrated Jumping Frog of Calaveras County* (1867)

Christian Science = *Christian Science**

Connecticut Yankee = *A Connecticut Yankee in King Arthur's Court**

Equator = *Following the Equator* (2 vols.)

Essays = *Literary Essays**

Europe = [James Brander, ed.], *Europe and Elsewhere* (1923)

Gilded Age = *The Gilded Age* (2 vols.)*

Hadleyburg = *The Man that Corrupted Hadleyburg, Etc.**

Huckleberry Finn = *The Adventures of Huckleberry Finn**

Innocents Abroad = *The Innocents Abroad* (1869)

Joan of Arc = *Personal Recollections of Joan of Arc* (2 vols)*

Man = *What Is Man? and Other Essays* (1917)

Mississippi = *Life on the Mississippi**

Roughing It = *Roughing It* (2 vols.)*

Sawyer Abroad = *Tom Sawyer Abroad, Etc.**

Sketches = *Sketches New and Old**

Stranger = [A.B. Paine, ed.], *The Mysterious Stranger, Etc.* (1922)

Tom Sawyer = *The Adventures of Tom Sawyer**

Tramp = *A Tramp Abroad* (2 vols.)*

Washoe Giant = [Franklin Walker, ed.], *The Washoe Giant in San Francisco* (San Francisco, 1938)

Wilson = *Pudd'nhead Wilson**

Other sources

Autobiography = A.B. Paine (ed.), *Mark Twain's Autobiography* (2 vols., 1924)

Biography = A.B. Paine, *Mark Twain: A Biography* (3 vols., 1912)

Carseres = Benjamin de Carseres (ed.), *When Huck Finn Went Highbrow* (1934)

Earth = Bernard de Voto (ed.), *Letters from the Earth* (1962)

Eruption = Bernard de Voto (ed.), *Mark Twain in Eruption* (1940)

Harnsberger = C.T. Harnsberger (ed.), *Everyone's Mark Twain* (1972 edn)

Henderson = Archibald Henderson, *Mark Twain* (London, 1911)

Honce = Charles Honce, *The Adventures of Thomas Jefferson Snodgrass* (Chicago, 1928)

Hornberger = Theodore Hornberger (ed.), *Letters to Will Bowen* (Austin, Tex., 1941)

Jest Book = Cyril Clemens (ed.), *Mark Twain Jest Book* (Kirkwood, Mo., 1957)

Johnson = Merle Johnson (ed.), *More Maxims of Mark Twain* (privately publ., 1927)

Kipling = Rudyard Kipling, *From Sea to Sea* (London, 1899)

Letters = A.B. Paine (ed.), *Mark Twain's Letters* (2 vols., 1917)

Life = Charles Neider (ed.), *Life as I Find It* (Garden City, N.Y., 1961)

Moments = A.B. Paine (ed.), *Moments with Mark Twain* (1920)

My Father = Clara Clemens, *My Father Mark Twain* (1931)

Notebook = A.B. Paine (ed.), *Mark Twain's Notebook* (1935)

Plymouth Rock = Charles Neider (ed.), *Plymouth Rock and the Pilgrims* (1984)

Read = Opie Read, *Mark Twain and I* (Chicago, 1940)

Sandwich Islands = G. Ezra Dane (ed.), *Letters from the Sandwich Islands* (Stanford, Calif., 1938)

Smith and Gibson = H.N. Smith and W.H. Gibson (eds), *Mark Twain-Howells Letters* (2 vols., Cambridge, Mass., 1960)

Speeches 1910 = A.B. Paine (ed.), *Mark Twain's Speeches* (1910)

Speeches 1923 = A.B. Paine (ed.), *Mark Twain's Speeches* (1923)

Wagenknecht = E.G. Wagenknecht, *Mark Twain: The Man and His Work* (New Haven, 1935)

Walker and Dane = Franklin Walker and G. Ezra Dane (eds), *Mark Twain's Travels with Mr. Brown* (1940)

Webster = S.C. Webster, *Mark Twain, Business Man* (Boston, 1946)

Wecter = Dixon Wecter (ed.), *The Love Letters of Mark Twain* (1949).

Life

All you need in this life is ignorance and confidence; then success is sure.   Carseres, 7

That kind of so-called housekeeping where they have six Bibles and no corkscrew.   *Notebook*, 210

Everything has its limit – iron ore cannot be educated into gold.   *Man*, 4

Let us not be too particular. It is better to have old second-hand diamonds than none at all.
Equator, I.xxxiv

Noise proves nothing. Often a hen who has merely laid an egg cackles as if she had laid an asteroid.
Equator, I.v

Reputation is the hall-mark: it can remove doubt from pure silver, and it can also make the plated article pass for pure.
Letters, II.472

Good friends, good books and a sleepy conscience: this is the ideal life.   *Notebook*, 347

The proper office of a friend is to side with you when you are in the wrong. Nearly everybody will side with you when you are in the right.   *Notebook*, 216

The thug is aware that loudness convinces sixty persons where reasoning convinces but one.
'Is Shakespeare Dead?' in *Man*, 354

You try to tell *me* anything about the newspaper business! Sir! I have been through it from Alpha to Omega, and I tell you the less a man knows the bigger the noise he makes and the higher the salary he commands.
Sketches, 314

Greatness may be classified as the ability to win recognition.
Read, 71

You have seen that kind of people who will never let on that they don't know the meaning of a new big word. The more ignorant they are, the more pitifully certain they are to pretend you haven't shot over their heads.
Connecticut Yankee, xviii

The irritating thing about ungoverned children is that they often make as orderly and valuable men and women as do the other kind.
Notebook, 266

The exercise of an extraordinary gift is the supremest pleasure in life.
American Claimant, vi

Often, the surest way to convey misinformation is to tell the truth.
Equator, II.xxiii

At certain periods it becomes the dearest ambition of a man to keep a faithful record of his performances in a book; and he dashes at this work with an enthusiasm that imposes the notion that keeping a journal is the veriest pastime in the world, and the pleasantest. But if he only lives twenty-one days, he will find out that only those rare natures that are made up of pluck, endurance, devotion to duty for duty's sake, and invincible determination, may hope to venture upon so tremendous an enterprise ...
Innocents Abroad, iv

Seventy is old enough. After that there is too much risk.
Equator, I.xxix

Certainly there is no nobler field for human effort than the insurance line of business – especially accident insurance. Ever since I have been a director in an accident-insurance company I have felt that I am a better man. Life has seemed more precious ... I do not care for politics – even agriculture does not excite me. But to me now there is a charm about a railway collison that is unspeakable.
Speeches 1923, 80

Happiness seeks obscurity to enjoy itself.
Read, 62

Praise is well, compliment is well, but affection – that is the last and final and most precious reward that any man can win, whether by character or achievement.

Speeches 1923, 343

I have no desire for riches. Honest poverty and a conscience torpid through virtuous inaction are more to me than corner lots and praise.

'A Cat's Tale' in *Earth*, 131

One thing at a time is my motto – and just play that thing for all it is worth, even if it's only two pair and a jack.

Connecticut Yankee, ii

Somebody has said that in order to know a community, one must observe the style of its funerals and know what manner of men they bury with most ceremony.

Roughing It, II.vi

That is just the way in this world; an enemy can partly ruin a man, but it takes a good-natured injudicious friend to complete the thing and make it perfect.

Wilson, v

We have not the reverent feeling for the rainbow that a savage has, because we know how it is made. We have lost as much as we have gained by prying into the matter.

Tramp, II.xiv

Always acknowledge a fault frankly. This will throw those in authority off their guard and give you opportunity to commit more.

Johnson, 5

It's an epitome of life – The first half of it consists of the capacity to enjoy without the chance; the last half consists of the chance without the capacity.

Letters, II.79

You cannot have a theory without principles. Principles is another name for prejudices.

Speeches 1923, 207

Well, well, a good and wholesome thing is a little harmless fun in this world; it tones a body up and keeps him human and prevents him from souring.

Joan of Arc, I.bk.II.xxi

A great and priceless thing is a new interest! How it takes possession of a man! how it clings to him, how it rides him!

Tramp, II.vi

The world will not stop and think – it never does, it is not its way, its way is to generalize from a single sample.

'The United States of Lyncherdom' in *Europe*, 239

Public shows of honor are pleasant, but private ones are pleasanter because they are above suspicion.

Hornberger, 26

...as happy as if she was on a salary.

Huckleberry Finn, xxi

Simple rules for saving money: To save half, when you are fired by an eager impulse to contribute to a charity, wait, and count forty. To save three-quarters, count sixty. To save it all, count sixty-five.

Equator, II.x

You can't depend on your judgment when your imagination is out of focus.   *Notebook*, 344

Only he who has seen better days and lives to see better days again knows their full value.

Notebook, 379

It is from experiences such as mine that we get our education of life. We string them into jewels or into tinware, as we may choose.

Biography, III.1277

There is an old time toast which is golden for its beauty. 'When you ascend the hill of prosperity may you not meet a friend.'   *Equator*, II.v

Do I seem to be seeking the good of the world? That is the idea. It is my public attitude; privately I am merely seeking my own profit. We all do it, but it is sound and it is virtuous, for no public interest is anything other or nobler than a massed accumulation of private interests.

Speeches 1923, 316

There is no sadder sight than a young pessimist, except an old optimist. *Notebook*, 385

Training is everything. The peach was once a bitter almond; cauliflower is nothing but cabbage with a college education. *Wilson*, v

For the majority of us, the past is a regret; the future an experiment. Read, 34

Age has taught me wisdom. If a spectacle is going to be particularly imposing I prefer to see it through somebody else's eyes, because that man will always exaggerate. Then I can exaggerate his exaggeration, and my account of the thing will be the most impressive.

'O'Shah' in *Europe*, 53

Grief can take care of itself; but to get the full value of a joy you must have somebody to divide it with.

Equator, II.xii

Intellectual food is like any other: it is pleasanter and more beneficial to take it with a spoon than with a shovel.

Tramp, II.Appendix D

To ask a doctor's opinion about osteopathy is equivalent to going to Satan for information about Christianity.

Notebook, 344

There is no such thing as a new idea. It is impossible. We simply take a lot of old ideas and put them into a sort of mental kaleidoscope. We give them a turn and they make new and curious combinations.

Biography, III.1343

I have found out that there ain't no surer way to find out whether you like people or hate them than to travel with them.   *Sawyer Abroad*, xi

The old saw says, 'Let a sleeping dog lie.' Right. Still, when there is much at stake it is better to get a newspaper to do it.   *Equator*, II.viii

Intolerance is everything for oneself, and nothing for the other person.   *Autobiography*, II.13

Leavin' me as happy as a dog with two tails.   *Honce*, 43

To hate her is an unspeakable luxury.   *My Father*, 84

Obscurity and a competence – that is the life that is best worth living.   *Notebook*, 298

Don't part with your illusions. When they are gone you may still exist but you have ceased to live.
                          Equator, II.xxiii

The holy passion of Friendship is of so sweet and steady and loyal and enduring a nature that it will last through a whole lifetime, if not asked to lend money.
                          Wilson, viii

We should be careful to get out of an experience only the wisdom that is in it – and stop there; lest we be like the cat that sits down on a hot stove-lid. She will never sit down on a hot stove-lid again – and that is well; but also she will never sit down on a cold one any more.
                          Equator, I.xi

[On duelling]: I think I could wipe out a dishonor by crippling the other man, but I don't see how I could do it by letting him cripple me.
                          Biography, III.1514

There is no character, howsoever good and fine, but it can be destroyed by ridicule, howsoever poor and witless. Observe the ass, for instance; his character is about perfect, he is the choicest spirit among all the humbler animals, yet

see what ridicule has brought him to. Instead of feeling
complimented when we are called an ass, we are left in
doubt.   *Wilson,* 'A Whisper to the Reader'

One values a thing when one can't afford it.
                        Christian Science, bk.II.vii

Water taken in moderation cannot hurt anybody.
                        Notebook, 13

The calamity that comes is never the one we had prepared
ourselves for.   Wecter, 317

To succeed in the other trades, capacity must be shown; in
the law, concealment of it will do.
                        Equator, II.i

It is your human environment that makes climate.
                        Equator, I.ix

Experience teaches us only one thing at a time – and hardly
that, in my case.   Harnsberger, 164

October. This is one of the peculiarly dangerous months to
speculate in stocks in. The others are July, January,
September, April, November, May, March, June,
December, August, and February.
                        Wilson, xiii

When your watch gets out of order you have choice of two
things to do: throw it in the fire or take it to the
watch-tinker. The former is the quickest.
                        Equator, II.xxviii

By some subtle law all tragic human experiences gain in
pathos by the perspective of time.
                        'My Literary Debut' in *Hadleyburg,* 84

Marriage – yes, it *is* the supreme felicity of life. I concede it.
And it is also the supreme tragedy of life. The deeper the
love the surer the tragedy. And the more disconsolating
when it comes.   *Letters,* II.811

Each person is born to one possession which outvalues all his others – his last breath.   *Equator*, II.vi

I think there is no sense in forming an opinion when there is no evidence to form it on. If you build a person without any bones in him he may look fair enough to the eye, but he will be limber and cannot stand up; and I consider that *evidence* is the bones of an opinion.

                    Joan of Arc, I.bk.I.ii

Familiarity breeds contempt – and children.

                    Notebook, 237

We have no permanent habits until we are forty. Then they begin to harden, presently they petrify, then business begins.   *Speeches 1923*, 257

First cuckoo I ever heard outside of a clock. Was surprised how closely it imitated the clock – and yet of course it could never have heard a clock. The hatefulest thing in the world is a cuckoo clock.   *Notebook*, 135

He was as shy as a newspaper is when referring to its own merits.   *Equator*, I.vi

Even the clearest and most perfect circumstantial evidence is likely to be at fault, after all, and therefore ought to be received with great caution. Take the case of any pencil sharpened by any woman: if you have witnesses you will find she did it with a knife; but if you take simply the aspect of the pencil, you will say she did it with her teeth.

                    Wilson, xx

Nothing is so ignorant as a man's left hand, except a lady's watch.   *Equator*, I.xxii

Spending one's capital is feeding a dog on his own tail.

                    Notebook, 345

There are those who scoff at the schoolboy, calling him frivolous and shallow. Yet it was the schoolboy who said, 'Faith is believing what you know ain't so.'

                    Equator, I.xii

Thunder is good, thunder is impressive; but it is the lightning that does the work.

Letters, II.818

The events of life are mainly small events – they only seem large when we are close to them. By and by they settle down and we see that one doesn't show above another. They are all about one general low altitude, and inconsequential.

Autobiography, I.282

It is easier to stay out than to get out.

Equator, I.xviii

We chase phantoms half the days of our lives. It is well if we learn wisdom even then, and save the other half.

Letters, I.150

There are two times in a man's life when he should not speculate: when he can't afford it, and when he can.

Equator, II.xx

[I] never smelt anything like it. It was an insurrection in a gasometer.

Connecticut Yankee, xx

A dozen direct censures are easier to bear than one morganatic compliment.

Equator, I.iv

I did not know then [when young], though I do now, that there is no suffering comparable with that which a private person feels when he is for the first time pilloried in print.

Mississippi, 1

...as scarce as lawyers in heaven.

'Information for the Millions' in *Calaveras County*, 144

The man with a new idea is a Crank till the idea succeeds.

Equator, I.xxxii

A soap bubble is the most beautiful thing, and the most exquisite, in nature ... I wonder how much it would take to buy a soap bubble, if there was only one in the world?

Innocents Abroad, xiii

He had had much experience of physicians, and said 'the only way to keep your health is to eat what you don't want, drink what you don't like, and do what you'd druther not.'

Equator, II.xiii

Optimist: Person who travels on nothing from nowhere to happiness.

Johnson, 11

Habit is habit, and not to be flung out of the window by any man, but coaxed down-stairs a step at a time.

Wilson, vi

None of us can have as many virtues as the fountain-pen, or half its cussedness; but we can try.

Equator, II.xxxii

Whoever has lived long enough to find out what life is, knows how deep a debt of gratitude we owe to Adam, the first great benefactor of our race. He brought death into the world.

Wilson, iii

Wrinkles should merely indicate where smiles have been.

Equator, II.xvi

A thing long expected takes the form of the unexpected when at last it comes.

Notebook, 236

I have traveled more than any one else, and I have noticed that even the angels speak English with an accent.

Equator, II.'Conclusion'

America

October 12, the Discovery. It was wonderful to find America, but it would have been more wonderful to miss it.
Wilson, 'Conclusion'

It does rather look as if in a Republic where all are free and equal prosperity and position constitute *rank*.
American Claimant, xii

They always go for our *manners*. Damn our manners – we claim no superiority there; we don't travel on our manners; they are no better than French ones ... The French for manners. They have contributed little else to this world – those and millinery styles – let them continue – for so God willed. But talk to us of our invention, energy, enterprise ... and our infamous politics.
Harnsberger, 345

I think that as a rule we develop a borrowed European idea forward and that Europe develops a borrowed American idea backwards.
'Some National Stupidities' in *Europe,* 175

Like all the other nations, we worship money and the possessors of it – they being our aristocracy, and we have to have one.
North American Review, 4 January 1907

When it comes down to pure ornamental cursing, the native American is gifted above the sons of man.
Roughing It, II.xix

We have a criminal jury system which is superior to any in the world; and its efficiency is only marred by the difficulty of finding twelve men every day who don't know anything and can't read.
Sketches, 235

The average American girl possesses the valuable qualities of naturalness, honesty, and inoffensive straightforwardness; she is nearly barren of troublesome conventions and artificialities; consequently, her presence and her ways are unembarrassing, and one is acquainted with her and on the pleasantest terms with her before he knows how it came about.

American Claimant, xx

Our papers have one peculiarity – it is American – their irreverence ... They are irreverent towards pretty much everything. *Notebook*, 195

July 4. Statistics show that we lose more fools on this day than in all the other days of the year put together. This proves, by the number left in stock, that one Fourth of July per year is now inadequate, the country has grown so.

Wilson, xvii

It is agreed, in this country, that if a man can arrange his religion so that it perfectly satisfies his conscience, it is not incumbent on him to care whether the arrangement is satisfactory to anyone else or not.

'As Regards Patriotism' in *Europe*, 301

We adore titles and heredities in our hearts, and ridicule them with our mouths. This is our Democratic privilege.

Autobiography, II.350

I think the reason why we Americans seem to be so addicted to trying to get rich suddenly is merely because the *opportunity* to make promising efforts in that direction has offered itself to us with a frequency out of all proportion to the European experience.

'What Paul Bourget Thinks of Us' in *Essays*, 155

A Southerner talks music.

Mississippi, xliv

That awful power, the public opinion of a nation, is created in America by a horde of ignorant, self-complacent simpletons who failed at ditching and shoemaking and fetched up in journalism on their way to the poorhouse.

Speeches 1923, 49

The American characteristic is Uncourteousness. We are
the impolite Nation ... It is only in uncourteousness,
incivility, impoliteness, that we stand alone – until hell
shall be heard from.   *Notebook*, 298

Even the foreigner loses his kindly politeness as soon as we
get him Americanized.   *Speeches 1923*, 300

It is a free press ... There are laws to protect the freedom of
the press's speech, but none that are worth anything to
protect the people from the press.

Speeches 1923, 43

It is by the grace of God that in our country we have those
three unspeakably precious things: freedom of speech,
freedom of conscience, and the prudence never to practice
either of them.   *Equator*, I.xx

Twain on Twain

I have been an author for 20 years and an ass for 55.

Biography, III.1277

I think I have seldom deliberately set out to be humorous, but have nearly always allowed the humor to drop in or stay out according to its fancy.

Biography, II.1100

I have never tried, in even one single little instance, to help cultivate the cultivated classes. I was not equipped for it either by native gifts or training. And I never had any ambition in that direction, but always hunted for bigger game – the masses. I have seldom deliberately tried to instruct them, but I have done my best to entertain them, for they can get instruction elsewhere.

Biography, II.894

After writing for fifteen years it struck me I had no talent for writing. I couldn't give it up. By that time I was already famous. The Twainian (May-June 1952), 4

I was always told that I was a sickly and precarious and tiresome and uncertain child, and lived mainly on allopathic medicines during the first seven years of my life. I asked my mother about this, in her old age – she was in her eighty-eighth year – and said: 'I suppose that during all that time you were uneasy about me?' 'Yes, the whole time.' 'Afraid I wouldn't live?' After a reflective pause – ostensibly to think out the facts – 'No – afraid you would.'

Autobiography, I.108

I was born modest, but it didn't last.

Speeches 1910, 137

Ah, well, I am a great and sublime fool. But then I am God's fool, and all His work must be contemplated with respect.

Biography, II.609

My books are water: those of the great geniuses are wine. Everybody drinks water. Notebook, 190

In the matter of diet – I have been persistently strict in sticking to the things that didn't agree with me until one or the other of us got the best of it.

Speeches 1910, 257

I was born lazy. I am no lazier now than I was forty years ago, but that is because I reached the limit forty years ago. You can't go beyond possibility.   *Eruption*, 256

If I cannot swear in heaven I shall not stay there.

Notebook, 345

I do that kind of speech (I mean an offhand speech), and do it well, and make no mistake, in such a way to deceive the audience completely and make that audience believe it is an impromptu speech – that is art.

Speeches 1923, 182

[When a reporter called regarding reports of his death with an order to write 5,000 words if very ill, 1,000 if dead:] You don't need as much as that. Just say the report of my death has been grossly exaggerated.

Biography, II.1039

I am never more tickled than when I laugh at myself.

Read, 60

Yes, even I am dishonest. Not in many ways, but in some. Forty-one, I think it is.   *Letters*, II.768

There ain't nothing more to write about, and I am rotten glad of it, because if I'd a knowed what a trouble it was to make a book, I wouldn't a tackled it and ain't a-going to no more.

Huckleberry Finn, 'Chapter the Last'

I came in with Halley's comet in 1835. It is coming again next year [1910], and I expect to go out with it. It will be the greatest disappointment of my life if I don't go out with Halley's comet. The Almighty has said, no doubt: 'Now, here are these two unaccountable freaks; they came in together, they must go out together.' [The comet appeared on 16 November 1835 and Twain was born fourteen days later on the 30th. It reappeared on 20 April 1910 and Twain died the next day.]   *Biography*, III.1511.

Literature, Writers & Critics

Literature is an *art*, not an inspiration. It is a trade, so to speak, and must be *learned* – one cannot 'pick it up' ... And its capital is experience. *Wecter, 228*

Experience is an author's most valuable asset; experience is the thing that puts the muscle and the breath and the warm blood into the book he writes.

'Is Shakespeare Dead?' in *Man*, 318

I don't believe any of you have read *Paradise Lost*, and you don't want to. That's something you just want to take on trust. It's a classic ... something that everybody wants to have read and nobody wants to read.

Speeches 1910, 194

I never saw an author who was aware that there was any dimensional difference between a fact and a surmise.

My Father, 86

We write frankly and fearlessly, but then we 'modify' before we print. *Mississippi*, xiv

Only one thing is impossible for God: to find any sense in any copyright law on the planet. *Notebook*, 381

I have a prejudice against people who print things in a foreign language and add no translation. When I am the reader, and the author considers me able to do the translating myself, he pays me quite a nice compliment – but if he would do the translating for me I would try to get along without the compliment. *Moments*, 139

I am not one of those who in expressing opinions confine themselves to facts. I don't know anything that mars good literature so completely as too much truth. Facts contain a deal of poetry, but you can't use too many of them without damaging your literature. *Speeches 1910*, 389

As a rule, the grammar was leaky and the construction more or less lame; but I did not much mind these things. They are common defects of my own, and one mustn't criticize other people on grounds where he can't stand perpendicular himself.

Connecticut Yankee, xxvi

To misplace an adverb is a thing which I am able to do with frozen indifference; it can never give me a pang.

Smith and Gibson, II.880

Get your facts first and then you can distort them as much as you please.   Kipling, 180

Cast iron rules will not answer ... what is one man's comma is another man's colon.   *Life*, 189

As to the Adjective: when in doubt, strike it out.

Wilson, xi

As soon as the Jubilee [of 1897] was over we went to what is called in England 'an hotel'. If we could have afforded an horse and an hackney cab we could have had an heavenly time flitting around.   *Europe*, 213

The Deerslayer is just simply a literary delirium tremens.

'Fenimore Cooper's Literary Offenses' in *Essays*, 96

Writing fashion articles, like wet-nursing, can only be done properly by women.

'The Lick House Ball' in *Washoe Giant*, 35

There are three infallible ways of pleasing an author, and the three form a rising scale of compliment: 1, to tell him you have read one of his books; 2, to tell him you have read all of his books; 3, to ask him to let you read the manuscript of his forthcoming book. No. 1 admits you to his respect; No. 2 admits you to his admiration; No. 3 carries you clear into his heart.   *Wilson*, xi

Prose wanders around with a lantern and laboriously schedules and verifies the details and particulars of a valley and its frame of crags and peaks, then Poetry comes, and lays bare the whole landscape with a single splendid flash.

Smith and Gibson, II.800

[Rudyard Kipling]: He is a stranger to me, but he is a most remarkable man – and I am the other one. Between us, we cover all knowledge; he knows all that can be known, and I know the rest.   *Eruption*, 311

[To William Dean Howells]: You make all the motives and feelings perfectly clear without analysing the guts out of them the way George Eliot does ... George Eliot and Hawthorne ... tire me to death. As for [Henry James'] *The Bostonians* I would rather be damned to John Bunyan's heaven than read that.   *Letters*, II.455

[Edgar Allan Poe]: To me his prose is unreadable – like Jane Austen's. No, there is a difference. I could read his prose on a salary, but not Jane's.

                                                    Letters, II.830

Damn the subjunctive. It brings all our writers to shame.

                                                    Notebook, 303

I like criticism but it must be my way.

                                              Autobiography, II.247

Experience has not taught me very much, still it has taught me that it is not wise to criticize a piece of literature, except to an *enemy* of the person who wrote it; then if you praise it that enemy admires you for your honest manliness, and if you dispraise it he admires you for your sound judgment.

                                                  Biography, I.506

'*Classic*.' A book which people praise and don't read.

                                                    Equator, I.xxv

How often we recall, with regret, that Napoleon once shot at a magazine editor and missed him and killed a publisher. But we remember with charity, that his intentions were good.   *Letters*, I.800

The critic assumes every time that if a book doesn't meet the cultivated-class standard it isn't valuable ... If a critic should start a religion it would not have any object but to convert the angels, and they wouldn't need it. It is not that little minority who are already saved that are best worth lifting up, I should think, but the mighty mass of the uncultivated.   *Biography*, II.894

Delicacy – a sad, sad false delicacy – robs literature of the best two things among its belongings: family circle narrative and obscene stories.

Letters, I.310

It is more trouble to make a maxim than it is to do right.

Equator, I.iii

The critic's symbol should be the tumble-bug; he deposits his egg in someone else's dung otherwise he could not hatch it.   *Notebook*, 219

[On reading a favourable review by William Dean Howells]: When I read that review of yours I felt like the woman who said that she was so glad that her baby had come white.   *Letters*, I.166

Truth is stranger than fiction – to some people, but I am measurably familiar with it. Truth is stranger than fiction, but it is because fiction is obliged to stick to possibilities; truth isn't.   *Equator*, I.xv

I have noticed, in such literary experiences as I have had, that one of the most taking things to do is to conceal your meaning when you are *trying* to conceal it. Whereas, if you go at literature with a free conscience and nothing to conceal you can turn out a book, every time, that the very elect can't understand.   *American Claimant*, v

The very ink with which all history is written is merely fluid prejudice.   *Equator*, II.xxxiii

I believe that the trade of critic … is the most degraded of all trades, and that it has no real value – certainly no large value … However, let it go. It is the will of God that we must have critics … and we must bear the burden.

Autobiography, II.69

We hate the critic and think him brutally and maliciously unjust, but he could retort with overwhelming truth: 'You will feel just as I do about your book if you will take it up and read it ten years hence.'   *Notebook*, 219

The Fine Arts

I used to worship the mighty genius of Michael Angelo …
But I do not want Michael Angelo for breakfast – for
luncheon – for dinner – for tea – for supper – for between
meals. I like a change, occasionally. In Genoa, he designed
every thing; in Milan he or his pupils designed every thing
… In Florence, he painted every thing, designed every
thing, nearly … He designed St Peter's; he designed the
Pope; he designed the Pantheon, the uniform of the Pope's
soldiers, the Tiber, the Vatican, the Coliseum … the eternal
bore designed the Eternal City, and unless all men and
books do lie, he painted every thing in it!

Innocents Abroad, xxvii

[On hearing Wagner's *Lohengrin*]: The banging and
slamming and booming and crashing were something
beyond belief. The racking and pitiless pain of it remains
stored up in my memory alongside the memory of the time
I had my teeth fixed.   *Tramp*, I.ix

It seems to me that to the elevated mind and the sensitive
spirit, the hand organ and the nigger [minstrel] show are a
standard and a summit to whose rarefied altitude the other
forms of musical art may not hope to reach.

Eruption, 110

Whenever I enjoy anything in Art it means that it is mighty
poor. The private knowledge of this fact has saved me from
going to pieces with enthusiasm in front of many and
many a chromo.   *Moments*, 282

I had seen the 'Mona Lisa' only a little while before, and
stood two hours in front of that painting, repeating to
myself, 'People come from around the globe to stand here
and worship. What is it they find in it?' To me it was merely
a serene and subdued face, and there an end. There might
be more in it, but I could not find it. The complexion was
bad; in fact, it was not even human; there are no people of
that color. I finally concluded that maybe others still saw in
the picture faded and vanished marvels which had been
there once and were now forever vanished.

'Down the Rhone' in *Europe*, 315

Women

A thoroughly beautiful woman and a thoroughly homely woman are creations which I love to gaze upon, and which I cannot tire of gazing upon, for each is perfect in her own line, and it is *perfection*, I think, in many things, and perhaps most things, which is the quality which fascinates us. *Autobiography*, I.323

A large part of the daughter of civilization is her dress – as it should be. Some civilized women would lose half their charm without dress and some would lose all of it. *Plymouth Rock*, 107

Heroine: girl who is perfectly charming to live with, in a book. Johnson, 8

There is nothing comparable to the endurance of a woman. In military life she would tire out an army of men, either in camp or on the march. *Autobiography*, II.116

'Have women a sense of humor?' an English friend once asked Mark Twain. 'Well,' replied the humorist, 'I don't think they have humor themselves, but they enjoy it in others. Now, you see that woman crossing the lawn there?' The woman was his wife. 'I don't suppose that woman ever said a humorous thing in her life; but she always sees the point of my jokes.' *Jest Book*, 27

To begin with, ladies are cowards about expressing their feelings before folk; men *become* cowards in the presence of ladies. *Notebook*, 200

Mark once argued the question of polygamy with a Mormon who insisted that polygamy was moral and defied him to cite any passage in the Scriptures that forbids the practice. 'Well,' queried the humorist, 'how about that passage that tells us no man can serve two masters?' *Jest Book*, 17

She had a beautiful complexion when she first came, but it faded out by degrees in an unaccountable way. However, it is not lost for good. I found the most of it on my shoulder afterwards.
Sketches, 197

[On a woman in man's clothing:] 'Well, I should say that lady is a perfect example of the self-made man.'
Jest Book, 10

[One husband] was reproached by a friend, who said: 'I think it a shame that you have not spoken to your wife for fifteen years. How do you explain it?' That poor man said: 'I didn't want to interrupt her.'
North American Review, 15 March 1907

Slang in a woman's mouth is not obscene, it only sounds so.
Johnson, 12

She was not quite what you would call refined. She was not quite what you would call unrefined. She was the kind of person that keeps a parrot.
Equator, II.xxi

Sport & Exercise

I have never taken any exercise except sleeping and resting, and I never intend to take any. Exercise is loathsome. It cannot be any benefit when you are tired; and I was always tired.   *Speeches 1923, 259*

I've been studying the game of golf pretty considerably. I guess I understand now how it's played. It's this way. You take a small ball into a big field and you try to hit it – the ball not the field. At the first attempt you hit the field and not the ball. After that you probably hit the air or else the boy who is carrying your bag of utensils. When you've gone on long enough you possibly succeed in obtaining your original object. If the boy's alive you send him off to look for the ball. If he finds it the same day, you've won the game.   *Jest Book, 32*

It were not best that we should all think alike; it is difference of opinion that makes horse-races.
                    Wilson, xix

It was the 10th of May – 1884 – that I confessed to age by mounting spectacles for the first time, and in the same hour I renewed my youth, to outward appearance, by mounting a bicycle for the first time. The spectacles stayed on.   *Speeches 1923, 109*

[On cycling]: Within the next five days I achieved so much progress that the boy couldn't keep up with me. He had to go back to his gate-post, and content himself with watching me fall at long range … Get a bicycle. You will not regret it, if you live.
                    'Taming the Bicycle' in *Man, 295*

Religion & Morals

All that is great and good in our particular civilization came straight from the hand of Jesus Christ.

Wagenknecht, 206

I looked as out of place as a Presbyterian in hell.

Biography, III.1395

And yet when you come to think, there is no real difference between a conscience and an anvil – I mean for comfort. I have noticed it a thousand times. And you could dissolve an anvil with acids, when you couldn't stand it any longer; but there isn't any way that you can work off a conscience – at least so it will stay worked off; not that I know of, anyway.

Connecticut Yankee, xviii

The truth is always respectable.

Tom Sawyer, xxiii

Always do right. This will gratify some people, and astonish the rest.

Eruption, 'Frontispiece'

Man proposes, but God blocks the game.

Harnsberger, 214

We ought never to do wrong when people are looking.

'Double-Barreled Detective Story' in *Hadleyburg*, 292

When in doubt, tell the truth.

Equator, I.ii

When Mark Twain was introduced as the man who had said, 'When in doubt, tell the truth,' he replied that he had invented the maxim for others but that when in doubt for himself, he used more sagacity.

Biography, III.1280

[He] is as happy as a martyr when the fire won't burn.

Webster, 123

He was not a direct liar, but he would subtly convey untruths.
Notebook, 325

When we repent of a sin, we do it perfunctorily, from principle, coldly and from the head; but when we repent of a good deed the repentence comes hot and bitter and straight from the heart ... In my time I have done eleven good deeds. I remember all of them ... I repent of them in the same old original furious way, undiminished, always.
Earth, 167

Truth is the most valuable thing we have. Let us economize it.
Equator, I.vii

Honesty is the best policy, but it is not the cheapest.
Smith and Gibson, I.57

Honesty: the best of all the lost arts.
Johnson, 8

Prosperity is the best protector of principle.
Equator, II.ii

Gratitude is a debt which usually goes on accumulating like blackmail; the more you pay the more is exacted. In time, you are made to realize that the kindness done you is become a curse and you wish it had not happened.
Autobiography, I.257

All say, 'How hard it is that we have to die' – a strange complaint to come from the mouths of people who have had to live.
Wilson, x

I have never seen what to me seemed an atom of truth that there is a future life ... and yet – I am strongly inclined to accept one.
Biography, III.1431

[Man's immortality]: Let us believe in it! ... It had been the belief of the wise and thoughtful for three thousand years; let us accept their verdict; we cannot frame one that is more reasonable or probable.
My Father, 177

The weakest of all weak things is a virtue that has not been tested in the fire.

Henderson, 192

To the pure, all things are unpure.

Notebook, 372

It seems to me that a man should secure the *well done, faithful servant*, of his own conscience first and foremost, and let all other loyalties go.

Speeches 1923, 123

A man that never believes in anybody's word or anybody's honorableness ... ain't got none of his own.

Sawyer Abroad, x

[He was] full of ... the serenity which a good conscience buttressed by a sufficient bank account gives.

Equator, II.xiii

Familiarity breeds contempt. How accurate that is. The reason we hold truth in such respect is because we have so little opportunity to get familiar with it.

Notebook, 237

India has 2,000,000 gods and worships them all. In religion all other countries are paupers; India is the only millionaire.

Equator, II.vii

If the desire to kill and the opportunity to kill came always together, who would escape hanging?

Equator, II.x

Few sinners are saved after the first twenty minutes of a sermon.

Hannibal Courier-Post, 6 March 1935

Religion consists in a set of things which the average man thinks he believes, and wishes he was certain.

Notebook, 153

Let us endeavor so to live that when we come to die even the undertaker will be sorry.

Wilson, vi

God puts something good and something lovable in every man His hands create.   *Speeches 1923*, 30

An uneasy conscience is a hair in the mouth.
                    Notebook, 392

The most outrageous lies that can be invented will find believers if a man only tells them with all his might.
                    Walker and Dane, 175

One must keep up one's character. Earn a character first if you can, and if you can't, then assume one. From the code of morals I have been following and revising and revising for 72 years I remember one detail. I could never use money I had not made honestly – I could only lend it.
                    Speeches 1910, 394

Do right *for your own sake*, and be happy in knowing that your *neighbor* will certainly share in the benefits resulting.
                    Man, 59

To be good is noble; but to show others how to be good is nobler and no trouble.
                    Equator, flyleaf

Each man is afraid of his neighbor's disapproval – a thing, which, to the general run of the race, is more dreaded than wolves and death.
                    'The United States of Lyncherdom' in *Europe*, 244

[The Mormon Bible] is chloroform in print. If Joseph Smith composed this book, the act was a miracle – keeping awake while he did it was, at any rate.
                    Roughing It, I.xvi

God works through man ... just about as much as a man works through his microbes.   *Biography*, III.1271

It is not worthwhile to strain one's self to tell the truth to people who habitually discount everything you tell them, whether it is true or isn't.
                    Eruption, 110

'Fear God and dread the Sunday School' exactly describe that old feeling I used to have, but I couldn't have formulated it.   *Letters*, I.274

The spirit of wrath – not the words – is the sin; and the spirit of wrath is cursing. We begin to swear before we can talk.   *Equator*, I.xxxi

The altar cloth of one aeon is the doormat of the next.
                                                                    Notebook, 346

There is a charm about the forbidden that makes it unspeakably desirable. The more things are forbidden, the more popular they become.   *Notebook*, 275

Golden Rule: Made of hard metal so it could stand severe wear, it not being known at that time that butter would answer.
                                                                    Johnson, 8

He cultivates respect for human rights by always making sure that he has his own.   *My Father*, 262

Never refuse to do a kindness unless the act would work great injury to yourself, and never refuse to take a drink – under any circumstances.   *Notebook*, 12

In all lies there is wheat among the chaff.
                                                        Connecticut Yankee, xi

There are several good protections against temptations, but the surest is cowardice.   *Equator*, I.xxxvi

If I had the remaking of man, he wouldn't have any conscience. It is one of the most disagreeable things connected with a person; and although it certainly does a great deal of good, it cannot be said to pay, in the long run; it would be much better to have less good and more comfort.   *Connecticut Yankee*, xviii

One of the most striking differences between a cat and a lie is that a cat has only nine lives.   *Wilson*, vii

The good and evil results that flow from *any* act, even the smallest, breed on and on, century after century, forever and ever and ever, creeping by inches around the globe, affecting all its coming and going populations until the end of time, until the final cataclysm.

'The Dervish and the Offensive Stranger' in *Europe*, 311

Duties are not performed for duty's *sake*, but because their *neglect* would make the man *uncomfortable*. A man performs but one duty – the duty of contenting his spirit, the duty of making himself agreeable to himself.   *Man*, 20

It is often the case that the man who can't tell a lie thinks he is the best judge of one.   *Wilson*, 'Conclusion'

There are 869 different forms of lying, but only one of them has been squarely forbidden. Thou shalt not bear false witness against thy neighbor.

Equator, II.xix

It was not that Adam ate the apple for the apple's sake, but because it was forbidden. It would have been better for us – oh infinitely better for us – if the *serpent* had been forbidden.   *Notebook*, 275

All the consciences I have ever heard of were nagging, badgering, fault-finding, execrable little savages! Yes: and always in a sweat about some poor little insignificant trifle or other – destruction catch the lot of them, I say! I would trade mine for the small-pox and seven kinds of consumption, and be glad of the change.

'The Facts Concerning the Recent Carnival of Crime in Connecticut' in *Sawyer Abroad*, 315

When all is said and done, the one sole condition that makes spiritual happiness and preserves it is the absence of doubt.   *Eruption*, 339

How I do hate those enemies of the human race who go around enslaving God's free people with pledges – to quit drinking instead of to quit wanting to drink.

Letters, II.459

When I reflect upon the number of disagreeable people
who I know have gone to a better world, I am moved to
lead a different life.   *Wilson*, xiii

Let us be grateful to Adam our benefactor. He cut us out of
the 'blessing' of idleness and won for us the 'curse' of
labor.   *Equator*, I.xxxiii

The girl who was rebuked for having borne an illegitimate
child excused herself by saying, 'But it is such a *little* one.'
                  'To My Missionary Critics' in *Europe*, 285

Do your duty today and repent tomorrow.
                                                    Johnson, 6

Make it a point to do something every day that you don't
want to do. This is the golden rule for acquiring the habit of
doing your duty without pain.
                                              Equator, II.xxii

Nothing so needs reforming as other people's habits.
                                                    Wilson, xv

Conscience, man's moral medical chest.
                                           Autobiography, II.8

But we were good boys ... we didn't break the Sabbath
often enough to signify – once a week perhaps.
                                           Speeches 1923, 251

The man who is ostentatious of his modesty is twin to the
statue that wears a fig-leaf.   *Equator*, II.xiv

A man will do *anything*, no matter what it is, to *secure his
spiritual comfort* ... A man cannot be comfortable without *his*
own approval.   *Man*, 17

The Christian's Bible is a drug store. Its contents remain
the same but the medical practice changes.
         'Bible Teaching and Religious Practice' in *Europe*, 387

Pity is for the living, envy is for the dead.
                                              Equator, I.xix

Apparently one of the most uncertain things in the world is the funeral of a religion.

Equator, II.xiv

[On the existence of heaven and hell]: I don't want to express an opinion. You see, I have friends in both places.

Henderson, 109

People pretend that the Bible means the same to them at 50 that it did at all former milestones in their journey. I wonder how they can lie so. It comes of practice, no doubt. They would not say that of Dickens' or Scott's books. *Nothing* remains the same.

Letters, II.490

A man should not be without morals; it is better to have bad morals than none at all.   *Notebook*, 237

It has always been a peculiarity of the human race that it keeps two sets of morals in stock – the private and real, and the public and artificial.   *Eruption*, 382

I was compelled to read an unexpurgated Bible through before I was 15 years old. None can do that and ever draw a clear, sweet breath again this side of the grave.

Biography, III.1281

Morals are an acquirement – like music, like a foreign language, like piety, poetry, paralysis – no man is born with them. I wasn't myself, I started poor. I hadn't a single moral. There is hardly a man in this house that is poorer than I was then.   *Speeches 1923*, 260

There is a Moral Sense, and there is an Immoral Sense. History shows us that the Moral Sense enables us to perceive morality and how to avoid it, and that the Immoral Sense enables us to perceive immorality and how to enjoy it.   *Equator*, I.xvi

Everybody's private motto: It's better to be popular than right.   Johnson, 7

Few things are harder to put up with than the annoyance of a good example. *Wilson*, xix

The easy confidence with which I know another man's religion is folly teaches me to suspect that my own is also.
Biography, III.1584

Conscience ... is that mysterious autocrat, lodged in a man, which compels the man to content its desires. It may be called the Master Passion – the hunger for Self-Approval.
Man, 98

In the matter of courage we all have our limits.
Speeches 1923, 386

Heaven for climate; hell for society.
Speeches 1910, 117

Be careless in your dress if you must, but keep a tidy soul.
Equator, I.xxiii

The universal brotherhood of man is our most precious possession, what there is of it.
Equator, I.xxvii

Mankind

Man is the Only Animal that blushes. Or needs to.

Equator, I.xxvii

Concerning the difference between man and the jackass; some observers hold that there isn't any. But this wrongs the jackass.

Notebook, 347

Human nature is *very* much the same all over the world; and it is *so* like my dear native home to see a Venetian lady go into a store and buy ten cents' worth of blue ribbon and have it sent home in a scow.

Innocents Abroad, xxiii

The human race consists of the dangerously insane and such as are not.

Notebook, 380

It is a *solemn thought*: Dead, the noblest man's meat is inferior to pork.

Johnson, 9

[He has] no more sex than a tape-worm.

Autobiography, I.75

Love seems the swiftest, but it is the slowest of all growths. No man or woman really knows what perfect love is until they have been married a quarter of a century.

Notebook, 235

But that is the way we are made: we don't reason, where we feel; we just feel.

Connecticut Yankee, xi

It is human to like to be praised; one can even notice it in the French.

'What Paul Bourget Thinks of Us' in *Essays*, 152

To be *busy* is a man's only happiness.

Letters, I.151

Circumstances make man, not man circumstances.
Notebook, 379

What sorry shows and shadows we are. Without our clothes and our pedestals we are poor things and much of a size; our dignities are not real, our pomps are shams. At our best and stateliest we are not suns, as we pretended, and teach and believe but only candles; and any bummer can blow us out.
'The Memorable Assassination' in *Man*, 170

We take a natural interest in novelties, but it is against nature to take an interest in familiar things.
Equator, I.xviii

[Mankind] is made up of sheep. It is governed by minorities, seldom or never by majorities. It suppresses its feelings and its beliefs and follows the handful that makes the most noise. Sometimes the noisy handful is right, sometimes wrong; but no matter, the crowd follows it.
Stranger, ix

Human pride is not worth while; there is always something lying in wait to take the wind out of it.
Equator, II.'Conclusion'

I believe that our Heavenly Father invented man because he was disappointed in the monkey.
Eruption, 372

We all do no end of feeling, and we mistake it for thinking.
'Corn-Pone Opinions' in *Europe*, 406

To create man was a fine and original idea; but to add the sheep was tautology.
Notebook, 379

'Bedouins!' Every man shrunk up and disappeared in his clothes like a mud-turtle. My first impulse was to dash forward and destroy the Bedouins. My second was to dash to the rear to see if there were any coming in that direction. I acted on the latter impulse. So did all the others.
Innocents Abroad, lv

When we remember that we are all mad, the mysteries
disappear and life stands explained.

Notebook, 345

Their very imagination was dead. When you can say that of
a man, he has struck bottom, I reckon; there is no lower
deep for him.   *Connecticut Yankee*, xx

Civilization is a limitless multiplication of unnecessary
necessities.   Johnson, 6

If a man doesn't believe as we do, we say he is a crank, and
that settles it. I mean it does nowadays, because now we
can't burn him.   *Equator*, II.xvii

I knew one thing – that a certain amount of pride always
goes along with a teaspoonful of brains ... and admirers
have often told me I had nearly a basketful – though they
were rather reserved as to the size of the basket.

Speeches 1923, 78

He lacks the common wisdom to keep still that deadly
enemy of a man, his own tongue.

Sandwich Islands, 116

We do not deal much in facts when we are contemplating
ourselves.

'Does the Race of Man Love a Lord?' in *Bequest*, 284

He liked to like people, therefore people liked him.

Joan of Arc, I.bk.II.xvi

It is not the least likely that any life has ever been lived
which was not a failure in the secret judgment of the
person who lived it.   *Notebook*, 385

The noblest work of God? Man. Who found it out? Man.

Autobiography, I.263

[Fear] It is a blessed provision of nature that at times like
these, as soon as a man's mercury has got down to a certain
point there comes a revulsion, and he rallies. Hope springs
up, and cheerfulness along with it, and then he is in good
shape to do something for himself, if anything can be done.

Connecticut Yankee, vi

When we do a liberal and gallant thing it is but natural that we should wish to see notice taken of it.

Joan of Arc, I.bk.II.vii

He had the supreme confidence which a Christian feels in four aces.

'Washoe, Information Wanted' in *Washoe Giant*, 62

Everyone has a dark side which he never shows to anybody.

Equator, II.xxx

He wasn't a very heavy weight, intellectually. His head was an hour-glass; it could stow an idea, but it had to do it a grain at a time, not the whole idea at once.

Connecticut Yankee, xxviii

The lack of money is the root of all evil.

Johnson, 10

We all have our shams – I suppose there is a sham somewhere about every individual, if we could manage to ferret it out.

Gilded Age, II.ii

Doctor Rice's friend ... came home drunk and explained it to his wife, and his wife said to him, 'John, when you have drunk all the whiskey you want, you ought to ask for sarsaparilla.' He said, 'Yes, but when I have drunk all the whiskey I want I can't say sarsaparilla.'

Speeches 1923, 245

If you pick up a starving dog and make him prosperous, he will not bite you. This is the principal difference between a dog and a man.

Wilson, xvi

By trying we can easily learn to endure adversity. Another man's, I mean.

Equator, II.iii

It is a dear and lovely disposition, and a most valuable one, that can brush away indignities and discourtesies and seek and find the pleasanter features of an experience.

Autobiography, II.171

If his modesty equaled his ignorance he would make a violet seem stuck up.

> *The Twainian* (January – February 1946), 4

Training – training is everything; training is all there is to a person. We speak of nature; what we call by that misleading name is heredity and training. We have no thoughts of our own, no opinions of our own; they are transmitted to us, trained into us. All that is original in us … can be covered up and hidden by the point of a cambric needle…

> *Connecticut Yankee*, xviii

Let us be thankful for the fools. But for them the rest of us could not succeed.

> *Equator*, I.xxviii

Neither a man nor a boy ever thinks the age he *has* is exactly the best one – he puts the *right* age a few years older or a few years younger than he is.

> 'Extract from Captain Stormfield's Visit to Heaven'
> in *Stranger*, 246

April 1. This is the day upon which we are reminded of what we are on the other three hundred and sixty-four.

> *Wilson*, xxi

There is nothing that saps one's confidence as the knowing how to do a thing.

> *Hannibal Morning Journal*, 23 April 1910

A man may have no bad habits and have worse.

> *Equator*, I.i

There are no grades of vanity, there are only grades of ability in concealing it.

> *Notebook*, 345

Learning began with talk and is therefore older than books. Our opinions really do not blossom into fruition until we have expressed them to someone else.

> *Read*, 38

You can't reason with your own heart; it has its own laws, and thumps about things which the intellect scorns.

> *Connecticut Yankee*, xx

Does the human being reason? No, he thinks, muses, reflects, but does not reason. Thinks *about* a thing; rehearses its statistics and its parts and applies to them what other people on his side of the question have said about them … He doesn't want to know the other side. He wants arguments and statistics for his own side, and nothing more.   *Notebook*, 307

Why is it that we rejoice at a birth and grieve at a funeral? It is because we are not the person involved.
                                        Wilson, ix

The timid man yearns for full value and demands a tenth. The bold man strikes for double value and compromises on par.   *Equator*, I.xiii

He would come in and say he had changed his mind, – which was a gilded figure of speech, because he hadn't any.   *Speeches 1923*, 139

Self-made man, you know. They know how to talk. They do deserve more credit than any other breed of men, yes, that is true, and they are among the very first to find it out, too.   *Connecticut Yankee*, xxxii

Man will do many things to get himself loved, he will do all things to get himself envied.   *Equator*, I.xxi

Courage is resistance to fear, mastery of fear – not absence of fear. Except a creature be part coward it is not a compliment to say it is brave … Consider the flea! – incomparably the bravest of all the creatures of God, if ignorance of fear were courage.   *Wilson*, xii

Man was made at the end of a week's work when God was tired.
                                    Biography, III.1195

We are always more anxious to be distinguished for a talent we do not possess than to be praised for the fifteen which we do possess.   *Autobiography*, II.139

Few of us can stand prosperity. Another man's, I mean.
                                        Equator, II.iv

It is not worth while to try to keep history from repeating itself, for man's character will always make the preventing of the repetitions impossible.   *Eruption*, 66

There isn't a Parallel of Latitude but thinks it would have been the Equator if it had had its rights.

Equator, II.xxxiii

One of the commonest forms of madness is the desire to be noticed, the pleasure derived from being noticed. Perhaps it is not merely common, but universal.

'The Memorable Assassination' in *Man*, 170

I will speak to him, though at bottom I think hanging would be more lasting.

'A Horse's Tale' in *Stranger*, 195

But we are all that way: when *we* know a thing we have only scorn for other people who don't happen to know it.

Joan of Arc, I.bk.II.xxiii

When people do not respect us we are sharply offended; yet deep down in his private heart no man much respects himself.   *Equator*, I.xxix

The human race consists of the damned and the ought to be damned.   *Notebook*, 380

Today I have been having an experience – and it results in this maxim: To man all things are possible but one – he cannot have a hole in the seat of his breeches and keep his fingers out of it.   Smith and Gibson, I.237

If there is any one thing in the world that will make a man incurably and insufferably self-conceited, it is to have his stomach behave itself, the first day at sea, when nearly all his comrades are seasick.

Innocents Abroad, iii

Human nature is the same everywhere; it deifies success, it has nothing but scorn for defeat.

Joan of Arc, I.bk.II.viii

He smiled all over his face and looked as radiantly happy
as he will look some day when Satan gives him a Sunday
vacation in the cold storage vault.

Eruption, 75

The only very marked difference between the average
civilized man and the average savage is that the one is
gilded and the other painted.   *Notebook,* 392

We are unanimous in the pride we take in good and
genuine compliments paid us, in distinctions conferred
upon us, in attentions shown us. There is not one of us,
from the emperor down, but is made like that. Do I mean
attentions shown by the great? No, I mean simply flattering
attentions ... We despise no source that can pay us a
pleasing attention – there is no source that is humble
enough for that.

'Does the Race of Man Love a Lord?' in *Bequest,* 274

You can straighten a worm, but the crook is in him and
only wanting.   Johnson, 14

We can secure other people's approval, if we do right and
try hard; but our own is worth a hundred of it, and no way
has been found out of securing that.

Equator, I.xiv

Manners & Society

Clothes make the man. Naked people have little or no influence in society. Johnson, 6

If you wish to lower yourself in a person's favor, one good way is to tell his story over again, the way you heard it.
Notebook, 345

It was only a little thing to do, and no trouble; and it's the little things that smooths people's roads the most, down here below. *Huckleberry Finn*, xxviii

It is easy to find fault, if one has that disposition. There was once a man who, not being able to find any other fault with his coal, complained that there were too many prehistoric toads in it. *Wilson*, ix

He had said she had red hair. Well, she had; but that was no way to speak of it. When red-headed people are above a certain social grade their hair is auburn.
Connecticut Yankee, xviii

Etiquette requires us to admire the human race.
Johnson, 7

In certain trying circumstances, urgent circumstances, desperate circumstances, profanity furnishes a relief denied even to prayer. *Biography*, I.214

Frankness is a jewel; only the young can afford it.
Letters, I.16

There are people who can do all fine and heroic things but one: keep from telling their happiness to the unhappy.
Equator, I.xxvi

Gossip of anykind and about anybody is one of the most toothsomely Christian dishes I know of.
My Father, 53

He called me a quadrilateral astronomical incandescent son
of a bitch.   Smith and Gibson, II.765

Agreeing with a person cripples controversy and ought not
to be allowed.
                    'A Little Note to M. Paul Bourget' in *Essays*, 170

Do not offer a compliment and ask for a favor at the same
time. A compliment that is charged for is not valuable.
                                                    Notebook, 380

Good breeding consists in concealing how much we think
of ourselves and how little we think of the other person.
                                                    Notebook, 345

A Banquet is probably the most fatiguing thing in the
world except ditch digging. It is the insanest of all
recreations. The inventor of it overlooked no detail that
could furnish weariness, distress, harassment, and acute
and long-sustained misery of mind and body.
                                                    Eruption, 320

To say a compliment well is a high art and few possess it.
                                                    Letters, II.685

He had a good memory, and a tongue hung in the middle.
This is a combination that gives immortality to con-
versation.   *Roughing It*, I.xxxv

When angry, count four; when very angry, swear.
                                                    Wilson, x

No real gentleman will tell the naked truth in the presence
of ladies.
            'Double-Barreled Detective Story' in *Hadleyburg*, 311

An occasional compliment is necessary, to keep up one's
self-respect ... when you cannot get a compliment in any
other way pay yourself one.   *Notebook*, 237

There are no people who are quite so vulgar as the
over-refined ones.
                                                    Equator, II.xxvi

[Concerning upstarts]: We don't care to eat toadstools that think they are truffles.   *Wilson*, v

None but an ass pays a compliment and asks a favor at the same time. There are many asses.   Johnson, 11

I don't remember that I ever defined a gentleman, but it seems to me that if any man has just, merciful and kindly instincts he would be a gentleman, for he would need nothing else in the world.   *Speeches 1923*, 283

Compliments always embarrass a man. You do not know anything to say. It does not inspire you with words ... I have been complimented myself a great many times, and they always embarrass me – I always feel that they have not said enough.   *Speeches 1923*, 362

Human nature is all alike ... We like to know what the big people are doing, so that we can envy them ... *conspicuousness* is the only thing necessary in a person to command our interest, and in a larger or smaller sense, our worship.   *Autobiography*, II.248

England & The English

With a common origin, a common language, a common literature, a common religion, and – common drinks, what is longer needful to the cementing of the two nations together in a permanent bond of brotherhood?

Speeches 1923, 34

[Westminster Abbey]: The moonlight gave to the sacred place such an air of restfulness and peace that Westminster was no longer a grisly museum of moldering vanities, but her better and worthier self – the deathless mentor of a great nation, the guide and encourager of right ambitions, the preserver of just fame, and the home and refuge for the nation's best and bravest when their work is done.

'A Memorable Midnight Experience' in *Europe*, 13

There is no such thing as 'the Queen's English'. The property has gone into the hands of a joint stock company and we own the bulk of the shares.

Equator, I.xxiv

The outlook [in 1897] is that the English-speaking race will dominate the earth a hundred years from now, if the sections do not get to fighting one another.

Equator, I.xiv

English afternoon tea is an affront to luncheon and an insult to dinner.   Harnsberger, 149

The English never play any game for amusement. If they can't make something or lose something – they don't care which – they won't play.

'The Million Pound Bank-Note' in *American Claimant*, 355

That beauty which is England is alone – it has no duplicate. It is made up of very simple details – just grass, and trees, and shrubs, and vines, and churches, and castles, and here and there a ruin – and over it all a mellow dream-haze of history.   *Equator*, I.xxix

[Englishman]: A person who does things because they have been done before. [American]: A person who does things because they haven't been done before.

Notebook, 169

The English are mentioned in the Bible: Blessed are the meek, for they shall inherit the earth.

Equator, I.xvii

The War [between the States] has brought England and America close together – and to my mind that is the biggest dividend that any war in this world has ever paid. If this feeling is ever to grow cold again I do not wish to live to see it. *Biography*, II.1064

Politics & Politicians

[On hearing of the death of a corrupt politician]: I refused to attend his funeral. But I wrote a very nice letter explaining that I approved of it.

Harnsberger, 473

No country can be well governed unless its citizens as a body keep religiously before their minds that they are the guardians of the law, and that the law officers are only the machinery for its execution, nothing more.

Gilded Age, xxix

If we would learn what the human race really *is* at bottom, we need only observe it at election times.

Autobiography, II.11

It could probably be shown by facts and figures that there is no distinctly native American criminal class except Congress.

Equator, I.viii

None but the dead have free speech.

Notebook, 393

What is the difference between a taxidermist and a tax collector? The taxidermist takes only your skin.

Notebook, 379

In statesmanship get the formalities right, never mind about the moralities.

Equator, II.xxix

A man must not hold himself aloof from the things which his friends and his community have at heart if he would be liked – especially as a statesman.

Connecticut Yankee, ix

The radical of one century is the conservative of the next. The radical invents the views. When he has worn them out the conservative adopts them.

Notebook, 372

Fleas can be taught nearly anything that a congressman can.   *Man*, 82

The despotism of heaven is the one absolutely perfect government. An earthly despotism would be the absolutely perfect earthly government if the conditions were the same, namely, the despot the perfectest individual of the human race, his lease of life perpetual.

Connecticut Yankee, x

A pretty air in an opera is prettier there than it could be anywhere else, I suppose, just as an honest man in politics shines more than he would elsewhere.   *Tramp*, I.ix

Senator: Person who makes laws in Washington when not doing time.   Johnson, 12

Reader, suppose you were an idiot. And suppose you were a member of Congress. But I repeat myself.

Biography, II.724

All gentle cant and philosophizing to the contrary notwithstanding, no people in the world ever did achieve their freedom by goody-goody talk and moral suasion: it being immutable law that all revolutions that will succeed must *begin* in blood, whatever may answer afterward. If history teaches anything, it teaches that.

Connecticut Yankee, xx

When politics enter into municipal government, nothing resulting therefrom in the way of crimes and infamies is then incredible. It actually enables one to accept and believe the impossible.   Harnsberger, 473

Let me make the superstitions of a nation and I care not who makes its law or its songs, either.

Equator, II.xv

Humour & Humorists

[Mankind] in its poverty, has unquestionably one really effective weapon – laughter. Power, money, persuasion, supplication, persecution – these can lift at a colossal humbug – push it a little, weaken it a little, century by century; but only laughter can blow it to rags and atoms at a blast. Against the assault of laughter nothing can stand.

Stranger, x

Humor is mankind's greatest blessing.

Biography, III.1556

Laughter without a tinge of philosophy is but a sneeze of humor. Genuine humor is replete with wisdom.

Read, 17

Humor is only a fragrance, a decoration ... Humor must not professedly teach, and it must not professedly preach, but it must do both if it would live forever. By forever, I mean thirty years ... I have always preached. That is the reason I have lasted thirty years.

Eruption, 202

[Humor] is the good-natured side of any truth.

Read, 34

Everything human is pathetic. The secret source of Humor itself is not joy but sorrow. There is no humor in heaven.

Equator, I.x

Humor must be one of the chief attributes of God. Plants and animals that are distinctly humorous in form and characteristics are God's jokes.

Biography, III.1556

What a good thing Adam had – when he said a good thing he knew nobody had said it before.   *Notebook*, 67

Humor is the great thing, the saving thing, after all. The minute it crops up all our hardnesses yield, all our irritations and resentments slip away, and a sunny spirit takes their place.

'What Paul Bourget Thinks of Us' in *Essays*, 163

I value humor highly, and am constitutionally fond of it, but I should not like it as a steady diet. For its own best interests, humor should take its outings in grave company; its cheerful dress gets heightened color from the proximity of sober hues.   *Biography*, II.1100

Travel, Europe & The Europeans

[Tourist guides]: They know their story by heart ... and tell it as a parrot would – and if you interrupt, and throw them off the track, they have to go back and begin over again ... There is one remark ... which never yet has failed to disgust these guides ... After they have exhausted their enthusiasm pointing out to us and praising the beauties of some ancient bronze image ... we look at it stupidly and in silence for five, ten, fifteen minutes – as long as we can hold out, in fact – and then ask: 'Is – is he dead?' That conquers the serenest of them.

Innocents Abroad, xxvii

They spelt it Vinci and pronounce it Vinchy; foreigners always spell better than they pronounce.

Innocents Abroad, xix

Just in this one matter lies the main charm of life in Europe – comfort. In America, we hurry – which is well; but when the day's work is done, we go on thinking of losses and gains, we plan for the morrow, we even carry our business cares to bed with us ... We burn up our energies with these excitements ... I do envy these Europeans the comfort they take. When the work of the day is done, they forget it. Some of them go, with wife and children, to a beer hall, and sit quietly and genteelly drinking ... others walk the streets ... others assemble in the great ornamental squares in the early evening to enjoy the sight.

Innocents Abroad, xix

I thought I would practice my French on him, but he wouldn't have that either. It seemed to make him particularly bitter to hear his own tongue.

'Playing Courier' in *American Claimant*, 493

France has neither winter, nor summer, nor morals.

Biography, II.642

It has always been a marvel to me – that French language; it has always been a puzzle to me. How beautiful that language is! How expressive it seems to be! How full of grace it is! And when it comes from lips like those [of Sarah Bernhardt], how eloquent and how limpid it is! And, oh, I am always deceived – I always think I am going to understand it.   *Biography*, III.1254

[Frenchmen]: Their gesticulations are all out of proportion to what they are saying.   *Notebook*, 216

The dance had begun ... Twenty sets formed, the music struck up, and then – I placed my hands before my face for very shame. But I looked through my fingers. They were dancing the renowned '*Can-Can*'.
                    Innocents Abroad, xiv

A person who has not studied German can form no idea what a perplexing language it is ... There are ten parts of speech, and they are all troublesome. An average sentence in a German newspaper is a sublime and impressive curiosity ... it treats of fourteen or fifteen different subjects, each enclosed in a parenthesis of its own ... finally, all the parentheses and re-parentheses are massed together between a couple of king-parentheses ... *after which comes the* VERB, and you find out for the first time what the man has been talking about ...
     'The Awful German Language' in *Tramp*, II.Appendix D

I can *understand* German as well as the maniac that invented it, but I *talk* it best through an interpreter.
                    Tramp, I.xiv

When I was talking (in my native tongue) about some rather private matters in the hearing of some Germans one day, Twichell said, 'Speak in German, Mark – some of these people may understand English.'
                    American Literature (March 1936), 50

In early times some sufferer had to sit up with a toothache, and he put in the time inventing the German language.
                    Notebook, 141

There is a great, a peculiar charm about reading news scraps in a language which you are not acquainted with – the charm that always goes with the mysterious and the uncertain. You can never be absolutely sure of the meaning … A dictionary would spoil it.

'Italian Without a Master' in *Bequest*, 289

Even popularity can be overdone. In Rome, at first, you are full of regrets that Michelangelo died; but by and by you only regret that you didn't see him do it.

Wilson, xvii

I stopped at the Benton House. It used to be a good hotel, but that proves nothing – I used to be a good boy, for that matter. Both of us have lost character of late years.

Innocents Abroad, lvii

Sayings Attributed to Twain

We all grumble about the weather – but – nothing is done about it.

Better to keep your mouth shut and appear stupid than to open it and remove all doubt.

When some men discharge an obligation you can hear the report for miles around.

The coldest winter I ever spent was a summer in San Francisco.

I take my only exercise acting as pallbearer at the funerals of my friends who exercised regularly.

When I feel the urge to exercise, I lie down until it passes away.

Giving up smoking is easy. I've done it hundreds of times.

I never let my schooling interfere with my education.

Don't go to sleep, so many people die there.

I became a newspaperman. I hated to do it, but I couldn't find honest employment.

There's nothing so annoying as to have two people go right on talking when you're interrupting.

I am pushing sixty. That is enough exercise for me.

When I was a boy of 14, my father was so ignorant I could hardly stand to have the old man around. But when I got to be 21, I was astonished at how much he had learned in 7 years.